POEMS from the PLASTIC BAG

poems from the plastic bag

Richard Eccles
illustrated by James Castleden

Published in the UK in 2015 by Red Hand Books

RED HAND BOOKS
Old Bath Road, London SL3 0NS
1618 Yishan Road, Minhang District, 201103 Shanghai
150th Avenue, Springfield Gardens, 11413 New York
Şerifali Mahallesi, Umraniya, 34775 Istanbul
Cross Road A, Andheri, 400093 Mumbai

www.rhbks.com

ISBN: 978-1-910346-13-6 (Paperback)

Printed and bound in the United Kingdom

To the memory of my Mother who
so lovingly disapproved

Contents

Introduction

Most poets don't write introductions, I've noticed, but maybe that's their problem. Just in case I've never met you and got to hear your who-you-are I'll tell you here a bit of how this lovely book came about and the parenting of these poems.

I have thought deeply of plastic bags. They are amazing things, with their catchy words written on and textures and strength and the way they stretch to accommodate whatever gets asked of them, like straining lungs or the shirt fronts of middle-aged men. I wear my plastic bag with pride, it's a badge of honour. All this nonsense about bags for life is just too clingy, too possessive. And, oh, the stuff of life that fills our bags: shopping, shoes, our moving-ins and moving-outs, our lunches, letters and our current books. When I see certain bags I'm reminded immediately of the book I kept in it and I get a pang for time that has gone forever and that period of my life when I kept that book in that bag. T S Elliot will always be in one of the Co-op's. And from there to the notebooks and the propelling pencils of my own writing and then the bits of paper when I didn't have a notebook. Everything got thrown into the plastic bag. Now it's time to see what's lurking in there.

And the first time I saw poetry performed live. Wow, I was blown away. By the badness. I was watching a friend perform some songs at an outpost of passive-subversive Yorkshire alternatives that served beer downstairs and let people sing and perform upstairs. When you consider the accomplishment of playing a guitar reasonably well, singing in tune and remembering the words in time with what you're playing you have to acknowledge the feat regardless of the quality or your taste in music. Whereas the poet was:

> Waving bits of paper, a bit like weighty Chamberlain,
> straining for the words, quite difficult to make out
> even by the writer whilst the listener's kept
> right out of the picture. I keep thinking of opera singers…

They couldn't even remember the lines that they themselves had written. No singing or playing, just bad mumbling of something with words in it. Surely I could do better? Surely?? It seemed a win-win situation. Write some outstanding lines, give up with the guitar and make everyone slap their thighs and listen. I was hooked. With the idea. I resolved to put into practice the principles outlined by my elocution teacher: speak loudly from the stomach and think of Julius Caesar addressing the troops. I stood up a week or two later and read out this poem above, waving my paper ironically. There's more of it but you don't need any more of it. No-one laughed of course, except out of sympathy. In fact, I had felt something at the time, as I was introduced and beckoned forward by the smiley compere, which I couldn't put into words for a while. I can now. Something akin to a wave of underwhelment goes rushing around the room when the hitherto relaxed crowd realise what's going to happen: a poet has risen to 'perform'. This can then be followed by another wave, much more visible as people assert their right to rise in groups and buy the next round at the bar. So much rising that I always get distracted. It's like a physics lesson in an inner city comp.

And the venues. The adventure is as much in the real world in which the poems are briefly given breath as much as in the imagined world of the poems themselves. Take nothing for granted. You might think person-stage-audience in a sort of in-front-of relationship type thing. But no, everything is different in Poetrytopia: as your sonnets are being sensitively delivered at ever increasing volume to compete with the swinging creaking doors of the kitchen and the chef bellowing out 'Five cod and chips, no mushies. Get a move on…' and the flock of Polish waitresses argue over whose table is whose, in Polish, then start shouting more because they think I'm shouting at them. Or at folk festivals trying to engage pensioners sitting on hay bales forty five feet away in a poetry competition from the side of an artic when all they've come for is to clack along to the Morris dancing whilst a half-insane drunken broken Geordie is fiddling at your feet with the mike stand and no one knows who he is or what he's doing. And there's a bar in Leeds where the 'performing space' is a gantry suspended twenty five feet in the air where the only contact with people is the tops of their heads and all they see is my waistband in a halo of disco lights. These were the maternity wards and the nurseries for of all my babies here. Almost all of them have been performed, often to death, literally, in such places as these.

Of course, there are the 'other' places; the poetry venues, the poetry slams, the cosy open mics and the poet's bedroom where it almost falls perfectly silent. The places where you might come along and really want to enjoy words used in playful, powerful and provocative ways. You might want to leave 3D HD multi-platform 4x4 iplaying PS3 or PS4 – and so dull – gadgo-theocracy behind, however briefly, for a simpler world with which nothing technological will ever compete, namely, people telling stories in poetry.

So, gentle reader, I leave you to flick, browse, delve or shout out the words reminding you as always how important you are, since the best of occasions demands the best of you, readers and listeners. One last thing: words on paper are not the same as words as sounds so there are some words in the form of pictures that have taken my little poems off on whole new ways I had never dreamed of. Thank you for listening.

RDE

Plastic
Bag

Trouser Suit

Remember the long hot summer of 1976? It didn't rain for whole months, it was like being abroad. And in spontaneous outbursts for no apparent reason everyone decided to take it all out on west coast American music and smug men with hair swarming around every facial orifice who could play the guitar really well. As if by magic in unspoken agreement one day we all thought the opposite of the day before and the Punk revolution exploded onto our streets and radios and televisions and record shops. And by god was it extraordinarily exciting if you were a teenager – safety pins, very dangerous hair, hugely uncomfortable plastic clothing that didn't resemble in anyway the cagoule, drainpipes with slashes, rips and slits and everyone playing the guitar really, really badly – in short, sex and danger everywhere in the air.

So my mother buys me, in response to these huge social changes, a pale mint two-piece trouser suit. I counted thirteen separate pockets; within the year I found another four secret ones. I think she got it from the Grattan catalogue. It took her eighteen months to pay for it at 15p a week. She'd still not got used to decimalisation and didn't realise 15p was nearly four shillings. It seemed a lot of money. For what you got.

None of these memories have ever left me.
I never found early love.

In the pet shop of emotions
the guinea pigs wear dungarees
they're running wildly rampagious
and doing it for themselves…

the seals are in the big pool
in cheap bikinis and stretchy thongs
having saturdaynightfeverfun
and splashing to summer's songs…

and there's cute little foxes that squeak 'n' peep
and some smooth slimy brutes in patterned slacks
that don't do much but burrow and snatch
like nuns at a car boot:

but Hark!
I hear the tiny dogs clomping about in their mega-trainers
scuffling and barking with the painted punks
and me
in my brand new pale mint two piece trouser suit
    in the pet shop of emotions
        am less wanted than the skunks.

Brother at Forty

'There's one thing you gotta get used to,' said Dad,
unexpectedly acting like a Dad, Mum in earshot
at St. Ambrose Barlow's St. Pat's Day dance
but the jiggy music's loud and thin as the caller's
raucous mike voice cuts us into shape…
and I drift back to then 'cos he was your age now
and I will see your face on your birthday
slowly turn with every meet-up every year
into the outline of our father, as if age
is pouring into every feature old beer
and you are slowly turning into something
you have come from; me too, the mirror
fills in all the bits that are still yours, not his
so we are a half a jigsaw, with a few too many pieces,
a photofit of lifted parts… you have his sometimes
staring-into-hell-and-infinity eyes that seem
so far from rest, you do his voice that makes me laugh
the careful layers of aging from fits of laziness
the head turning to contradict before inertia sits back in…
and what do you see back? His nose,
the mocking mouth too quick to open, the hurt
of incomprehension in those around,
the muscle twitches around the lips
articulating everything of the little left unsaid.
It's hard to impart the disappointment

he must have felt on the scene back then
on me at fifteen. Perhaps he saw himself too much.
It's hard to ever travel away from this genetic track.
It's hard to see me in you and him in us
without knowing now his despair, his long
trailing off into his long unbeing.
But on the dance floor, years ago
he passed a gem of wisdom to his son
from a father, empty of love:
'There's one thing you gotta get used to, son…
dancing with the beer swilling in your belly.'
Something we've both done well, bro,
the one thing we've done really well.

Witty Things Overheard in the Golf Club Between December and May

As part of my political and social conscience I aim to reflect very much the language of modern Britain by listening carefully to the detail of what people around me say. And having spent a lifetime studying linguistics I have almost no friends left. Consequently, the textual nuances of this poem have been discussed in several learned journals as they have detected historical resonances concerning golf club banter that go right back to the very beginning of Britain. It's called, Witty Things Overheard In The Golf Club Between December And May. I will be attempting to play more than one character in this poem. Thank you.

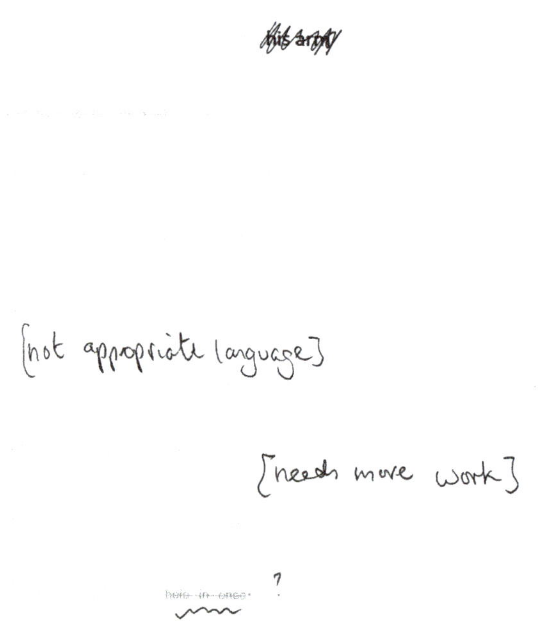

Thank you, I don't always get it right. This poem is also one of my most successful in old people's homes.

from Smithfield Urinals Tapestry, ca. 1403

The Waiting Room

At the intersection in time and space of the bus stop and the dentist's waiting room your whole life and the last third of human history passes before your eyes and your teeth are dealt with. Unfortunately you are still alive. Very near are people with half a pound of metal in clamped mouths hanging on for the next bus into town.

The waiting room. Understatement.
The interminable room only more terminal.
The room where people who have outwitted death wait.
The folk who dream of a train or a bus.
Romantics who have bought the drugs
from Boots and believe in eternal youth.

In the waiting room a fly is born.
Somewhere a mollusc dies.
We think, from upstairs, we hear the cries
from a make-do maternity ward
of a brand new traveller in God's world
or the prayers of the Count of Monte Cristo
opting to wait for a bus without the needle
or it could just be the drivelling souls
of the Restless Undead in the corridors
of the Hall of Customer Relations Advisors,
hovering just off the floor and re-living
aloud all the best tales of the times when the bus didn't come…
and above the inhuman squeals and hums
only the sounds of the rattling chains of the author
of the Passengers' Charter…

Out of the blue an ancient Grandma in her two hundredth year
draws a picture for her fractious fifty year old granddaughter
of a thing like a train, but we shudder at the hint in the picture
of it turning up on time with a bit of momentum:
'Dissembling clack-dish, a pox on't, 'tis the work of Satan!'
shouts a patron helping a travelsick maiden
to the toilet, and the shout goes up, Black Death! Black Death!
for peasants travelling on buses and trains
got pock-marks and pustules, boils and bursting organs
so the Government stepped in and privatised the symptoms,
that was 1349 and it's still claiming victims
so we pass round a nosegay for a long protective sniff.

The sun sets and the sun also rises.
The medics come and wheel out the corpses.
A voice like a human scratches the speaker.
The words are like real ones only bleaker.
Then a jingle, an advert and above the dentists' drills
rises a sound we've never heard.

A thing quite like an engine.

Thong One: Prelude Organum

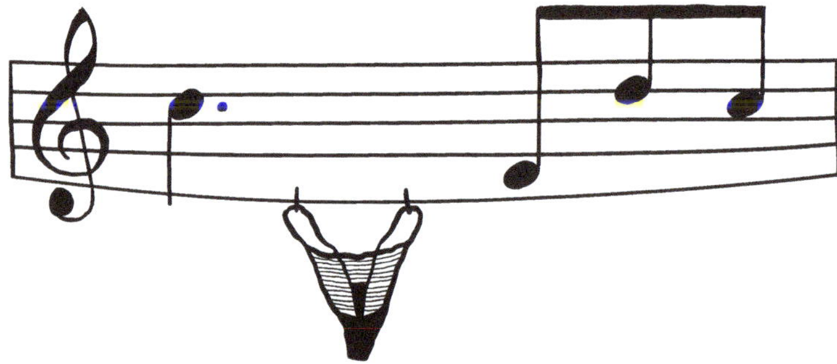

I am very interested in thongs. Statistically thongs are always present in any given throng, but would you ever admit you were all thonged up if you were dared to share your wearing in public? As part of my research I have been watching important studies on Channel 5, called Club Reps Revealed, or something like that, and there's absolute proof on the telly that almost everyone is either wearing a thong or not wearing a thong replacement. Even the parents who are spying on their kids on other important television studies are wearing thongs as the TV companies want to split families up in order to make follow-up programmes about Britain's Most Split Families.

I am proud to present to you here the world's most important collection of poems about the thong, The Thong Cycle. These pieces can also easily be read the other way round as The Cycle Thong, cutting down on washing. The collection bears important similarities with major musical forms and is thus divided just like a Sympthongy, into four parts. Each one of these parts touches parts the other parts don't touch, but there is overlap of material. Similar to Sibelius' obsession with b-flat.

The Fishfryer's Thong

I always wanted greasy hair and to inherit a fish shop but I didn't want to work in it… this poem presents an enviable mix of the typical fish finish and the powerful emotion of sexual attraction. I wrote this on a note and passed it to the lady behind the counter. She wrapped my two cod and a sausage in it.

A bit of fish before the batter
but there's always something the matter.
Will she order fillets, bits or scraps?
His heart gets the battering.
He's all fingers and thumbs
wiping up the dripping trap.

Senior Manager's Thong

Man at the top, what a racket!
If it talks out of turn, bloody sack it!
Just look at me and my rocket in my packet!
Come on, boys, faces to anuses
come up smiling with back to back bonuses
there's a thousand openings to fill your trousers
even my thong's got a pair of big pockets,
and if it's trough to snout I'm open all hours
me thong's so stuffed it's got a new placket.

Thong Haiku

Two lines cut and trimmed
One long line in the middle
Plotting the angles

The Tramp's Thong

A travelling man is always wearing his washing.

Hitler's Thong

I like short poems… they give you more time for television… this one attempts to bridge the gap between Emmerdale and the fridge…

What with one jackboot in Russia
and the other stretched out across North Africa
is it any wonder
the Third Reich went to cock in the bunker?

'The God-Of-Who-You-Sit-Next-To' Blues

Just look at yours and yous
across the tables of lovely booze
through the fug of fags
and shared times past.
Why's you with them lads,
muckers, mates, old pals –
them missuses, wives or bits of flooze,
toyboys, old flames and the latest squeeze
partners, lovers or losers at the next door chair?
Even the saddoes and the George Clooneys
know we're sitting next to our own… life stories.

First school is where the blues begin
boy girl boy girl boy girl boy girl
from purgatory to a Catholic school
where I sit side by side with hell and sin:
girl girl girl me girl girl and a thing…
who threw me round the room and bullied me in country dancing
and I hid when I heard myself called the kid who sits
next to the smelly kid.

Big school meant daft Maffit,
a cleft palate and a Thunderbird's head like Troy,
this wasn't Saturday Night With Parkinson
and worse when I looked round the room
boy boy boy boy boy boy another thing and me

Just look at yours and yous
it's Wednesday night, it's music 'n' booze
there's looks and touches, smiles and lies
we've fallen out or we're hypnotised
there's dazed and confused and morning glory…
even Ivana Trump and Asda's workers
know we're sitting next to our own… life stories

First love was courtesy of National Express
at twenty you think you have eternity,
I only had Bradford to Skegness:
Dora was an older woman and she wasn't coming back
row twelve, aisle seat, one in front of the toilets
and Dora, if you're out there, do you still have the beach huts
and those other things that aren't regrets?

But things change – deckchairs folded,
chairs covered and re-upholstered,
in my religion there's a lot more fun
in the library than on the internet:
trains and planes but **not** automobiles –
'cos you usually know them who's in them –
so burn your season tickets
cancel the cosy corner in the restaurant for romantics
and sit round the brazier with any protesting pickets
and don't leave the house without a set of shooting sticks.

So, just look at yours and yous
and ask yourself, did you really choose
the person you're sat next to?
If you sat down together to muse
could you write a little hymn to
him… or her… your very own
The God stroke Goddess of who you're sitting next to blues?

Try the bingo on your own
shout 'house' whenever, then move round
you just can't lose…
and after ten on a Saturday night
try A&E or the ambulance crews
and ask them who they've just sat next to…
But even I have proof
that the God exists of who you're sitting next ta
'cos my best friend who only I can see
is clever and he's called Dexter.

Beautiful Tea-towels

It was the most prosperous invention the Devil ever set on foot for the promotion of idolatry.
Thomas Paine

It's all very well saying 'post-industrial society'
when you mean the mess of our towns
the fucked-up boarded-up cocked-up factories
and the shouted-down looted shut-up lackeys
living with the spillage of decaying silently

from your star-studded TV studios or
your Headboy's arse-polished front bench
or well-heeled conference platform speaker
as remote and packaged and cushioned
and as far from the truth
as a Dalek with a wet-wipe is from a PE teacher

but when you're down there,
listening to it, thatcher blather major blather
blair blather and now another one
carry on cameron blather blather blather
but while you're down there, love, wipe this up
and give us your change from your minimum wage
waiting for the bus, the benefits, the telly to change
Brucie to die on a Saturday night. Summat.
Anything.
Something to change the blather the clapping and the frocks
as remote unwashed, dismantled and rattled

as vacuous as the wind in the boarded-up house
that's had the vandals round
you were right, Maggie, it's just postsociety
same as postbox, just a word that's empty

It's all very well saying 'that's the way it's always been
you can't change it, it just won't work, not the sort of thing that fits the Brits',
in that gutsy Queen-Mother-in-a-blitz of clichés pub and parlour way,
but what's very just and fair and true and very, very historical
that one man owns Cornwall and thirty more
of the bloated-up sort are having all your cream and your cake and eating it
too and you're doing their washing up
in that appropriate parlour maid way

But when all's said and done at the end of the day
you get what you deserve, yours is the short straw,
suck it and see cos we've just made clichés law
for all the Britains who've put their brains on Ebay

Well I say, let's have more titles, let's be more fair:
for creative use of spraycans and a hundred minor public disorders
let's give the Duke of Asbos Warwickshire and his mates two shires more
and the Prince of E's from the middle of Leeds
has given more pleasure than Prince Charles with all his weeds
here's Highgrove, good gardens for roaches, buttons and horse

let's put our trust in beermats adorned in union jacks
and rip down the car parks to make way for the cuts

put your pensions in serviettes and hearts and coronets
put up some laws where the factories once stood

and buy celebrity bibs embossed with national hymns
and pass on more laws to the babies on their nappies

more words less mess more lords more workloads
and free dusters for all the dodgers on benefits

we're in it together to wipe out all thought
more words for less, get one buy three

more cuts more opinions tax opinions tax toil
less brain more fat for kitchen accidents use kitchen royal

for god's sake more pageant pomp and hail
for Her Majesty, The Most Absorbent Queen of Post-UK
drivel arrayed in popular souvenir tea-towels.

Transit

I try to think of some of the people who never get poems about them. This is Mr. White Vanman and Ms. van Battery, formerly Vanman, estranged. They are out there. You might be surprised how tender this one is but it is truer than a lot of newspapers.

Everywhere is an emotion
passing through it there is a Transit
and the same Transit Vanman
driving in it
compelled motion behind the faded fascia
and piled-up pining papers
and the plastic holder once
held a tax disc in it
and just a dog lead curled up
in the footwell
of a dog left somewhere
no-one's fault, is it.

Somewhere in a soggy flat
going slowly apart
driven out of her mind
is the long-left lass
of the transitory man
wants their kid once
to get a card from his dad
wonders if any thoughts ever swerve
round a corner of his head

mirror him in the headlights
make him brake
slow down
pull up
stop him looking for his one true love
Brenda the dog
who got the same name as his mum.

On Being a Brummie... Poet

There's a fair few, possibly unfair many, raised eyebrows,
if you're honest at hearing a Brummie… err, poet…

I was going to stop there, 'cos it's sort of funny, in it
everything you say… if you're a Brummie… poet, err,
yeah, you heard it

It's as if I've got my dipthongs on the wrong way round…
and everything's constricted
and cutting in to come out through the wrong hole
… me nose… so, err, something's afflicted
and it's got alien written through it…

There may be life out there but not with accents as we know it
so with a government grant and an offpeak buspass
setting out into the farthest reaches of the vocal system the Brummie poet,
armed with the International Phonetic Alphabet,
where the starship of the vocally distressed can orally go
to take samples from planets like Acocks Green,
probe hostile Sarehole in molten middle earth,
and clock the locals in the frozen wastes of Nechells and gasless Perry Barr,
and just up the road is Deritend, an a pre-solar nebula
right at the end of the galactic donut
(though Solihull is still a star too far)
he hops on hops off with samples on his tape recorder

from them aliens what can copolt a conversation:
the evidence from the local life-form is not the ball-curdling drop
of a laryngeal dental fricative pile-up
or a vowel-sized hole filled with asteroid-shaped adenoids

and backwards facing comedy heads of backwards unemployed droids.
Bring it back to earth, with a bang, ma'am, please:

Sow wat if woy sai tarrarabit,
n hers gorra cobb on and garron me wick
after a fyow points o lager tops everyone gets kaylied
a catch the buzz up the booza n loyv the mowta without the air
n disapphear up an all oy where all them kidz are pushin buggiz,
who've got rowz n rowz of babbiz…

We could easily be humans.

Not quite like that type of pratt
who speaks in a put-on, funny, Brummie accent… oroyt?
at any point within one hundred yards –
funny and fine for the first four and a half hours
of strangled-vowel mockery
until the switch is flicked in the sensitive soul
who reaches out to grab him ever so gentloy
by the ball of his larynx –
just wish he had the two – and squeeze him like a psoycho
'Listen pal, only woy can tek the michael'.

Thong Two: Hommage Rondo

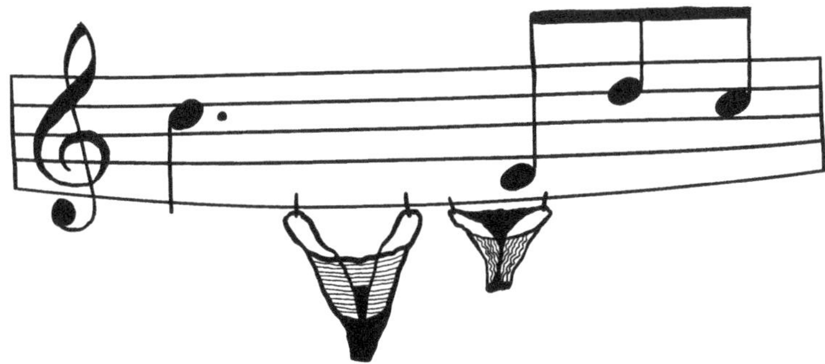

As part of my ongoing exposition of thongs I had invited a number of people round to my house as part of a discussion group to get more hands on with Thongs in a Cultural and Historical Setting but take the vibe up several notches to a socially relaxed atmosphere with wine, some cheese sandwiches and whatever anyone fancied bringing, and really try to clamp down on any illegal substances but still keep it really academic and potentially publish our findings in any willing magazines or on the internet. Despite threats of being removed from chatrooms by the female invitees we managed to achieve a quorom at our first meeting, just the two of us, me and Brian, taking our lead from UKIP by starting very, very small and also Wilberforce. Talking of forces, I have had a tip off that Brian is an undercover policeman.

When I looked up on Wikipedia what Hommage meant it certainly was way beyond me so I will leave that one with you. But it's certainly true that in loads of places around the world where anthropologists are doing excellent work in new excavations, everyday conversations are revealing that it seems absolutely fine to cut off someone's head and eat their eyeballs and smear their brains all over your latrine as a mark of disrespect but one thing is absolutely certain – you never touch their thong, not even when you have dismantled every other part of their cadavres and fed it to the dogs. This must go right back to pre-Genesis times. These poems are conforming to this ancient thinking.

Blair's Thong

Here's one that's slightly old hat, but not as old hat as the war in Iraq… it's called Blair's Thong. This is a historical poem composed in 1743. For those of you who are not familiar with this period in history Tony Blair was President of England and also a cruel dictator who ate foreign babies.

Something's wrong, there's a lasting piece missing,
But a top new position with all this coming and going
As a tightly-packaged envoy
Can't patch it up…
All these years on, Tone,
And your Bush is still showing.

The Unknown Soldier's Thong

Blown up out of all proportion

Leder Thongen

Ein zwei drei vier
Ich musse Handen putte hier
inside meine Furlinen
in Winterlederhimmel'n,
ist bische stiv mein Leder
und Schmallwintervinkelshrinker
wann man looser ganger
in meine kampe Pfants!
Danke Gott fur der Furherliner!

Mao Tse Tung's Thong Twisters

Offering a lot of support on the Long March

A Caveman Has a Vision of Breakfast Time in the Middle Capitalist Period

In this powerful scene a caveman foresees a domestic breakfast scene nearly 150,000 years into the future which reminds him of how good things are in his own life. He is happy going out to work to kill things in brutal acts of bloodthirsty violence but realises this can't continue as a career option forever. This can be a very useful lesson or not, depending.

Hairless Man makes sound like Mammoth:
I don wanna gooooooooooooo

Woman makes sound like two hissing sticks:
Hhhhphhphssssssberk

Man makes sounds like dying dog:
You don't understand… I donnnnnn wannna gooo

Woman makes sound like speaking to Hairless Baby:
Here lunchpack. Mammothmeat. Good. Old. Chew now, ready for lunch.

Hairless Man makes sound like first time thinking kill something:
Woman not listen. Don't like mammothmeat. What happen when kill mammoth? Eat mammoth. What happen when kill woman? No lunchpack.

Hairless Man makes sound like first time connect brain and mouth:
Uuuurghh. I see you in a week. I need time to think.

Strange Trade

Just popped into the Co-op
for some bread for toasting,
plain food after a bad bout
of diarrhoea and vomiting,
so glad after two days in bed
to be freed of the bug
of the bog-gripping kind
to mooch over sickly buns,
reduced stuff and sickening
scenes of drought in the savannah
on The Independent's angry
face…
… time's up, time to queue and pay,
but the cashier's hidden for ages,
and behind her stacks
of razors and booze and ciggies
and pills for killing yourself
like Anadin and Steradent
and jars of coffee…
'Jars of coffee? Jars of coffee?' I'm asking
everyone in the queue, so long the door's ajar,
cold air rushing in.
'We have to put it there
otherwise they nick it, sell if for a quid in the pub…'
Sounded so aufe, she did, with criminals' tricks,
'But,' I said, '… it's Nescafe…
why don't they nick the Fair Trade stuff
and give good taste a chance?'

Royal Wedding, England's Veg

We can't afford a flagpole round where I live so I'm starting the Sausage of Love Campaign by hanging a suitable porker out of my window and getting myself a large pork pie and a can of alcohol-free austerity Cheeky Vimto to join in the fun with two people I don't know, every time something like this happens.

Loyal in my jerkin,
I am Turnip,
proud yeoman of Engalond
ruddy in maiden-bedding,
parsnip-proud and ready
for a right royal tear-jerkin.

Plant me ten beds down
I is the brain of pea
willing to die for royalty
in fairy-tale Slumberlond
bellowing the shiter wail of pale,
we is potatoes kept in the dark
but all un-bagged and given flags
along the royal joyful vegetable route.

Indigestion

I'm sorry about my script I had to pester this drunk on the train before he lent me it... A concrete poem is one where the shape reflects the content. My concrete poem this evening is Indigestion and my chosen form tonight is the Oesophagus – that's the bit where food goes, for anyone who isn't a doctor – this bit down here is the appendix and I cut out about 60m of stomach and most of the rectum...
Concrete poem – very important to remember that...

Big and meaty This riff of burps Like Megadeth...with acid
B – b – buh – bah – bur - beoorrghh!!
This rift valley gullet Washing up liquid
Just like washing up liquid
Why's all this plastic Engulfing me mastics Tasting of ejaculates
Coming up and eyeing me?
It's an airport novel of sex and death, It's completely unputdownable
Or Chris de Burgh's Embarrassing back {fart} catalogue,
Match of the Day's Repetitive analysis – It's hell on earth –
The unending conga classes,
Scotch eggs
Countdown
Ranting
And gripping
It's repetitive
And gripping
It's lists
And politics
It's the sickening
Appendix
to having a good time

Next week's concrete poem is The Duck.

Big and meaty
This rift of burps
like Megadeth with acid
B - b - b - b - beorgghh!
This rift valley gullet
washing up liquid
Just like washing up liquid.
Why's all this plastic
engulfing me mastics
tasting of ejaculates
coming up and eyeing me?
It's an airport novel of sex and death
it's completely vnputdownasce
or Chris de Burgh's fart
embarassing back catalogue
Match of the Day's
repetitive analysis –
it's hell on earth –
the unending Conga clanes
scotch eggs
Countdown
ranting
and g[illegible]
it's repetitive
and gripping
it's lists
and politics
it's the sickening
appendix to having a good time

Thong Three: The Shepheardes Calenderes Thonges, Twelve Songs of Frolicking for High Voices

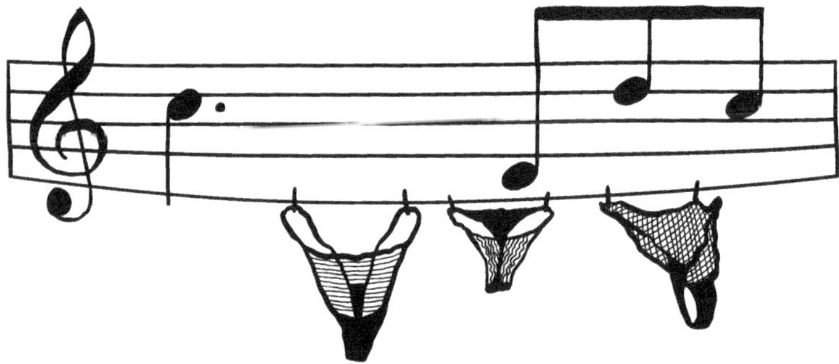

It sometimes seems a little pointless to study English literature so here is a shortcut to a very dull poem that covers more or less the same points: Things could have been a lot worse because The Shepheardes Calender is mercifully short compared to The Faerie Queen which is about a posh English rough bloke who comes to terms with his gayness in Elizabethan New York whilst fighting the Irish but not in this poem.

Here we meet a young shepherd called Colin Clout who has huge aspirations which he wants to make known to a wider public. In my original research into Colin's magical year many unknown aspects of mediaeval dress – very tight and lots of green – and also some of the big-hitting ditties of the Dit Parade have been here revealed for the first time.

I hope I have captured the power of love in the music in these poems which was originally written for 12 voices and water cannon. Some people have noticed quite loudly the similarity of my music to that great song, Get Off The Stove, Grandma, You're Too Old To Ride The Range but I am stating categorically that these songs are a lot older than that one. And better.

The Shepheardes Calenderes Thonges

January

A shepherd lad got out his pipe
thinking of naught but nice ditties
he'd led his flock on yon bleak hill
but fearsome Boreas blew his will
his branch was wilted and his stalk
half-broke so he could barely walk
and so he parks his feeble flock
behind a hedge and puts his head
in the bosom of an ancient's limbs
so he put away his instrument
with a dream of a popular lay.

February

Old shepherd's brag of wearing out thrice thirty thongs a year,
old bullock's boast is venteth into long and windy ears
wherupon young shepherd playeth air-piping in his hoodie head
And hearing wise sayinges againe he pulleth the cloth round his eares.

March I

April is the tighteste monthe
whan folk longen to goon on diete.

March II

Shepherd boys are strung along their crooks with maiden's looks
Seeing not the crack of love is paining but parting gets them off the hooks.

April

And there good Gawain, gay clad and Gaynore ful-thonged in throng upon the dais
and roll of drums and dainties plying on pipes ful shrill and al amongst the gayest
and Colin steals in, our shepherd boy, to peer anon at the realm's big peers
when al at once a champion thrice twice the size of a garderobe appears
with belly and waist most fitly formed and so square and cheek so sharply cut and clean
and never seen such tightly drawn hose all striped in fashion bright but too much green.
But Colin, marry, saw the dames
all swoon with lusty longing
for of all the knights he alone
strode around without a-thonging.

May

No cuttinge corners in lufes triangels.
Colin lufeth Rosalind and alswo Alysoun
and Colin hadde lisp whan singing thongs
and only one lady laughed out loud.

June

Up at the crack of dawn to whistle to young lambs
and pipe ditties idyllic under spreading boughs
brushing off annoying flies and tramps
the young shepherd hath made fulle his vows
to leaven this full dulle thong of land and job
and to finde summe mutton y-dressed as lamb
and blow her away with his bagpiping.

July

And for forty dayes he strode so proud
away from all he knew but the folks he found
along the way some be lewde some alle be schrewde
go shrewes where they go and where he sang he did get booed
upon all the streets and concert grounds.

August

And for two forthnights he frequenteth taverns more lowly
and he found not true love beneth the gerdell of the lovely
for his station was so lowly and they ofte him tolde
to take his pipe and chove it where his thonge blowe.

September

And Colin sees some come in countenance of clothynge disguised
and in prayers and penaunce putten hemselfs al for the love of Our Lord
and so he doeth doen do the same and selleth all his pieces of cloth,
excepten one but now tieth his thong round his head.

October

Folk flock to see fantasies like japeres and jangleres
but nothing compares from upon his rock to Colin's lady's wares.

November

All folks keep flocking to watch Colin's nothing but Bishops are very wary
so they send the soldiers to pull him down and cast him out of town
and make him wear something called braies that won't pull the crowds in.

December

Winter drawes on seems foolish in a thong for the shepherd without hus or clouthes
so Colin fares home but a Pole's tooke his job minding the flockes
and he wissen not what but to live back with his mam and claimeth doles.

Feeders at the Human Zoo, or genius loci laboris

Preening like a classical hairstylist
in a peacock's gown
a figure fawning disarmingly
with the libation bowl
stooped so low forever in clay
relief to feed the ego
the frailest suckling the strongest
in the ritual tableau
as sickening a sight for travelers
in the ancient world
as watching girls slaughtered at a funeral
all this on view
every day for the visitor to the zoo
of the sacred cults at the offices
please all gods, come god, go god
it matters not
the smiles are for the afterlife
the pension in the hereafter
the cornucopia
passed from paw to paw
the actors playing animals
playing tiny gods
filling the parts
written by Narcissus.

Ringing The Dead

I remember once ringing the dead
with a stick I found on the beach
whilst I poured sand on my granddad.

The stick itself I saw it shift
and a hand from the sea lift it
out as I made grandad's last bed.

And the beach itself was full of folk
and I asked the dead to stop
the waves come near my grandad's head.

It took a while before they replied,
and when my shadow shortened
I fed my granddad with all our bread,

I laid the food out just as they said
all finely left as he slept,
fare and fodder for the crossing ahead.

They said whoever sees the stick
must take care for they are next
and tell the dead their wordless names instead.

And from her deckchair in the sun
I saw my grandma's eye open.
She saw the stick. It made my heart sick

that they would want another one.
Once you ring the dead the peace
is ended, everywhere is keening.

The Share

At the end of the day a woman makes incisions
with a flint on the wall of a cave:
a v for days of blood,
a line to mark the dry.

The men together paint before the hunt,
prefigure the chase and the butchery,
but leave the victor indistinct, they cannot
over-measure the spirits' work.

When they are gone the women gather
and count out portions and tasks, experiment with water,
grain and chaff, note the lengths of shadow and grass,
mark half the time until men will return.

The men are blind to everything before the kill
except the coming blood spurting over hands
and who will claim the prize. No reckon what the moon,
the spirits and the women will count for theirs.

Five Poems About Adultery

Adultery can be a really good spectator sport with elements of a crime novel – whodunit quickly followed by whydunnit – and the same rules as cage fighting then often finished off with a bit of audience involvement and a phone-in along the lines of a Big Brother vote to see who gets thrown out of the House. Of course it's not funny but there's a lot more of it going on than half the people in any audience know about.

And don't let anyone tell you it's not about the sex. You might call it passion or love but it's 98% wild, insane sex that's just about to cost you your real partner, your house, your friends and your self-respect, if you've got any left and survive that far. Some experts would add job, car and hair.

These poems are about the other 2%.

Oystercatcher

We arrive here out of the blue. Trespassers
beware, history is in the air.
Unpasteurised light puckers
the brow. There are cracks and lips
in the spray-wet rocks for the witless
and unsuspecting.

Out on the sea to the untrained
eye heads of seals and dragons rise
for air between swells, but staring
unblinking, catch the tangled limbs
of kelp and seaweed rooted
like hanged men.

Why do people come to the edge
like this? You have to shout three
times, bend in the wind for breath,
open-eyed in the raw.
With a foot the washed-up
dead bird is turned for closer
inspection. We'll remember
his markings for the book.

Only now when I am putting down
these words am I aware of the look.

of the dead bird, a name, only, the beady
one with the unmoving head,
a northern Mona Lisa, eyes always
there. Our kneeling at the shallow
pools, the levering of the limpets,
resorting to kicks. The looks. The uneven,
heavy shift of weight jerking.

The stories have such gaps
and are such fragments catching us
in our retelling, between the surf gather,
the rise and run and the hammer of the innocent
shore, whipped as well by the wind.
The true story is in between.

The oystercatcher is oblivious.

Last House Before Dark

What did January beach up on your step
one wavering afternoon, between rain
and snow, black clouds, in a backwash
tripping up the beachcomber
acting as householder?

Two times nine now as I write the steps
how the fluctuating pattern of moon
and tide, pulling down, sucking in cycle
shingles and sand, the hidden insides
of faltering finder and keeper.

In the bone-white light off the winter
sea, the first of many firsts in wave
between wave, hand does before the words,
plaiting stone on your bedroom sill with ribbon
of fluttering future:

I hobble out to the brig, scared to slip
into christening fonts of rock pool
wariness, you float at home, I
crab, make you laugh out loud, squirming
before our first landlady.

A moon shrinks and someone asks
for seeds, your porno-petalled
hollyhocks ringing your doorway
begging envy. First firm 'no' to Jack
the lad, bean-stalker, rover.

At the first of separations, I leave
you for just a moment, scribble hasty,
lusty words in lines and slip in between
a tiny see-through V in lace.
First froth ever, you say, from anyone.

First time, they say, is eternal,
all circumstances inscribed. Adultery's
the same, nothing after is ever the same.
Suddenly the last's in sight, the flame
is split, reflection leaves a stain.

Last hour before morning light, making
coffee for one, last time the bleary-eyed
wife asks what's wrong, in dressing
gown. First time you've told a truth
in twelve months: 'nothing 'cept with me'

Last blurred breath before the ocean.
The voices flash like lighthouses,
the magnetic push against the anti-
gravity of light and oxygen
the drowning man, not waving, escaping.

Down the lane, under second summer
trees, green depths, the air is
heavy as sea-water I must push
through. Too long in the sun and parched
the terrace appears and drifts

in focus, out. Someone's holding
my breath, pressing me down, diverting
my eyes. I've only seconds left
to climb the depths for first air
like something converting gills

to lungs. First cries, what's lost,
first shape on dry lips, kissing dust,
I've come (no sound) to you, just shape
and baggage, as old as Odysseus,
last house, last home, where your light is
last harbour before the dark.

Paper Hat

The days are jumbled and the memory so free,
the lines of winter clearer, summer still a haze,

but the garden dry, the grass humbled in the heat,
only single expectant insects flitting near,

even the swallows twitter pinned into the eaves,
our idling chatter skittering 'cross the well,

you disturbing with fingertips the surface,
me drawing water with my hands, more spilled than held

and through my fingers you come shimmering,
blue and white, mesmerising in a paper hat.

Slowly turning in your glare, the novelty glows
between us but my fingers replace the delicate

fibres of lacy flare and brim with velvety
mouth and skin. You will not remember. Drop the stone,

we won't sense all the ripples or what the water
touches before the stillness is restored. One last

thing – the man you were with staring at 451 degrees.

Nelly's Tale

Nelly was a horse living in the west of Ireland and out of the blue I was presented with a band woven from the hair of her mane, of the sheerest black I have ever seen. Certain sorts of people noticed it and their reactions were often vociferous and fetishistic, which can be disconcerting when you are sitting on a bus reading quietly. I saw it in other terms, as here.

These are the delicious after-moments,
after ruin and destruction: smoke
from charred embers, way-off moans
and sobs, dust and blood and memories too
vivid in the flash of annihilation.
Then the quiet. and this delicious, lingering
of re-collection.
what happens to cities after their fall?

We agreed the treaty, one line:
'no fear of death'.
Take off, departures, no turning
to look back. Leave-taking, mouthing
what is forbidden, last thing
on the lips, maybe forever, who can say?

What was it like before?
In the streets of our town like any other,
exchange, clamour,
the goods and chattels of love passed back and forth
and in the squares and the taverns

the dancing, the flowers and the conversations
say spring, spring is here
there is nothing to fear.

The downfall is in the detail.
Who would have seen the shift of
the wind still full of western beaches,
hawthorn drenching us in corpse's trace,
our wisest starting stories and strange
to hear them falter
and laughter deep and catching
like fire, even though we kept all-night
moonlit vigils, and hammered out love
as hard as the best of our blacksmiths –
no weapons, no guards, no foresight,
no names can ward off this guile:
sweetwitch. Shadowless. Bluegaze.

Below the city walls, a simple token,
left, woven from a mare's tail,
a band in three parts, in equal
measure black switch and weft
and weightier than gold in any torque,
fitting the wrist, riding the cuff,
pulled on, tied and sealed – too late
now to close the gates. When night comes
we will know our fates, knowing this
was no trick of the mythical horses.

Witching

You are my book of visitors,
mixing owl-wise and lightning
in listing what really was what.

You are my corkscrew and my oyster,
promising, clammed, but prizing
out the sparkle and the dirt,

the night's prize-giving, the full red
carpet, the MC, the hurt
bright boys so willing in roster.

You are the yellow, the grey, the jaded
green courtesan licking ice-cream,
acting pretty, sitting in a poster.

You are the safe hand and the silkworm,
the devourer and the spinner,
you feeding with love what you wrought.

You are deeply the uneasy thought
the gnawing of bones in dreams,
the shades behind the moonlit lane.

But you are most the Rectifier,
the witch who decides who burns, who leads
the same one endlessly to fire.

as if the time and date screwed and bolted
every moment, but how would you ever know
about the space I've left for a title forever so
but still with time to go back to, memory

jolted, telling our tales and fixing sense to experience:
there is something of the church in the mechanic's
workshop, God is in the motors, somewhere sticks
or runs but not quite right, it's obvious the history

of mis- or over-use to those dexterous ears
taking apart the many parts in their 3D minds,
locating a carburettor adjustment by divine
right, sensing straight through the plastic covers,

hearing the poor spark, the unoiled chain, pistons
and compression not matching the equations
of the manufacturer. they do so well approximations,
on paper everything seems so different, existence

sometimes like deciding to become the faulty
machine and suffer adjustments and possible
replacements or assume the role of the foibled
human repairer envisaging oneself, the difficulty

flitting between the two, knowing what turns
want, how to screw down or up the ego
or spark the id, thinking through what ergo
sum becomes, running constantly, long winters,

cold starts and taking care for granted.
this state of mind that was is soon long
gone, 'I want…' 'I was…' sometimes just the song
of the exhaust, lost fuel, echo of a haunted,

forgotten need to turn the motor, set the chain
in motion, cut as proof of the interminable
existence, agitate instead of reason, label
me by becoming different. opposites remain.

and so, the dislocation of the smallest parts
is the emotion, what comes out of, presumably,
motion, so I pick out the prime mover of, presumably
these connections: the title's in the space of hearts.

Thong Four: Opera Buffa

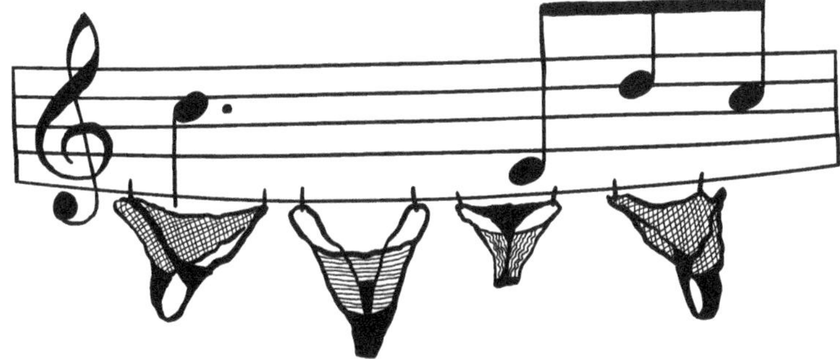

When the heart stirs and the emotions rise and the sense of the world's grandeur is erupting in a man's innermost places listening to the power of the climactic crescendos of the finest music ever written, for example, in one of Beethoven's operas, it is easy to see the similarities between this and getting your outfit just right: the feeling of looking like you are riding the wave.

Begin with the basics, get the fundamentals right and you will breeze through the day knowing you look good and everything's sitting pretty. You can mix and match a paisley tie with a stripey shirt and a businessy white zipper thong or if slacks are your thing for the summer heat and you're going from pay-check-savvy and office hours to happy hours a fully-lined blazer-type thong to soak up the sweat is this season's must have. Think Beethoven but funk him up with matching leather clutch bag. Be yourself, the thong remains the same.

Quasimodo's Thong

In memoriam et in voce Leslie Phillips

I say – DING DONG!
It's a ver ver spectacular sight!
The Hunchback's banging is splitting the night
the blighter's hanging on in the tower in a bit of a show
and rather a palaver from his tortured bells
but there's a message in his ding of woe
there's a story in his dong of love
the song is wrong, the ding all tinny
it's more than a tinkle escaping the cathedral.
Steady on, old bean! Stiff upper lip!
But the rope's got caught as he shoots from the hip
he's trailing off, he's thrown Esmerelda over
now he's dropping down like a bat out of hell
his bells are bashing Paris' cobbles.
The bells, the bells! he just wouldn't be told.

The Ageing Bridegroom's Thong

Constraint in front, a certain looseness expected behind
and above a waistband of gold
holding it all in
place. Love's hanging scales slightly sunken.
The Aging Bridegroom must constantly re-adjust.

Thug's Thong

Haaaaaaaaaaaard,
harder than a pair of walnuts.
He doesn't crush nuts, he glasses other nutter's nuts
then eats three packets of Nobby's Nuts
and then the empty foil packets, dust 'n' all. Guts of steel!
So hard he has no regrets.
When he was at school
he put two shot putts in each trouser pocket
and his mam brayed him when she found out.
There's nothing he doesn't put in his mouth.
Nothing much ever comes out.

Don Juan's Thong

Missing In Action

At the Temple of Horus

'Halloooo…' more allelulia or call to prayer
from the hawker actor in the war
of wares, Act One, scene four, Opera
on the Boats: picture cardboard
set of Middle Nile, palms, kids and lots of water,
the big guy's moving centre stage…
'Hallooo, Rambooo' – he must mean
me behind the gunwales, an orator on green
baize waving towels bringing me down
with irony to earth from the gods
bobbing on prows, as good as princes
playing Falstaff in watercolour gowns…

'Yes, sister… you understand?' audience
participation in the ancient survival
pantomime… **'me down, you up, half you,
ten for me, ten for you, last price…'** Act Two,
scene three, early exit threat with scarves just to scare
the very wary… **'lady give me fair
price, two piece for you…'** sung not shouted,
waving not waning, just a beginning, an opening.
You, sister, are Ophelia, ensnared.

Middle of the show is fated flaws
what you cast is what you reap
projection is everything: tablecloths or robes
'No harm to see, you look you see'
plastic-bagged projectiles
bombard Nile-bound Eve
under siege and laughing in bikini,
unaware of Isis' sifting fury
collecting all her murdered
husband's bits from riverwater,
except the national treasure, the penis of Osiris.
It all happens in this story.

A beginning a muddle and no end,
one rowing just so one stands still,
no doubting Hamlets or demanding soliloquy
just give good money, quid pro quo.
'Come, mister, two for one, beautiful lady
...ten no good, give me twenty, ten no...'
and Eve unbags the jalabah and wears it for Cleopatra
no such thing as doing much about nothing
his King Leary face surpasses his last natural
cry of, **'Sisters sisters'** and all the betrayal,
at home all his children crying
everywhere the desert edging the Nile
while the gods prevail always in denial.

The GM Dartboard Needs a Haircut

I wrote this for the heads of state at the G8 conference and this bloke who wouldn't let me on a train last week from London.

When you think about change and progress no one would have guessed that compared to the 1950's ninety per cent fewer of us have gabardines.

This poem came to me in a dream but I couldn't get the words out, so my friend wrote it for me. He's having a new kitchen fitted and he understands being possessed. And it's true, apparently we share seventy per cent of our DNA with a cabbage. I'm not sure about that, there's evidence he says that where he lives that figure is rising dramatically…

It's round and it's got feelings
it's found in mounds and it's got meaning
it's closer to me than my family
it shares with me its DNA…
so seventy per cent or more
of you and me is cabbagey.
So the scientists say.

But what if it went
just one per cent
the other way?
And I got greener, it got pinker –
quick, give me God back –
'cos evolution's

suddenly a stinker –
one small step for a cabbage
could mean it's got short legs
and I'm stuck
on the couch
getting balder and glossier.

And if we've been here
just for the blink
of an eyelid
and dinosaurs
are only a burp away,
what's one per cent more or less,
like interest rates they sneak
up and unbalance you
and before you know it
seventy is seventy-five
and it'll have eyes
and need my glasses
and I'll be asking
it to read to me
from the newspaper.
It'll all go quiet
while it clears
its voice,
shifts in its seat, peers…
over my glasses,
starts with something safe

and avoids
the science reports
and I'll be content
with shrinking ears,
Pot Noodles
and the football pools.

It'll want Frosties for breakfast
and to operate the curtains
plan its viewing
from the Radio Times,
and as we chat over
Hobnobs and a nice cup of tea.
The greedy cabbage
is getting rather tactless,
says I'm becoming tasteless,
the only place I blossom
is the steam room
but no-one else
can bear the smell…
suggests I keep my head down,
don't look over the rim of the pan,
'cos the cabbages
are adding bits of people
to themselves
and throwing darts at the
hairy GM dartboard.

education

Hairmare, or a Brand New Poemover

I first discovered the value of shouting around the age of two but was promptly slapped and told not to do it again. But now I am up on a stage I can draw on that experience as a two year old and shout quite loudly in the manner of a poet. Or a madman banging on about the Bible.

This is my Hairmare, my vison of a new path of the righteous which shall come to pass as Poemover, where the words are stretched to cover the gaps left by the limited nature of the follicular growth:

'And it shall be proclaimed that hair is a sin against humanity...'

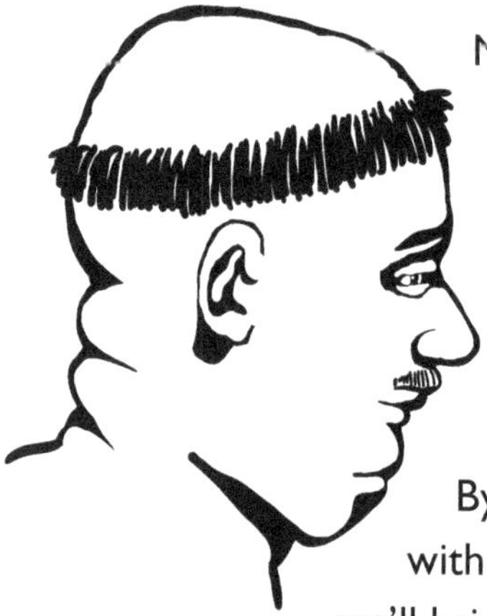

No more staring at bouffant daring,
no more shouting – Oi, Baldy! – without everyone turning round,
no more wondering is the glass half full or the head half empty,
for the sake of health and safety
the end is nigh for all our hair
and all our hairy paraphernalia.

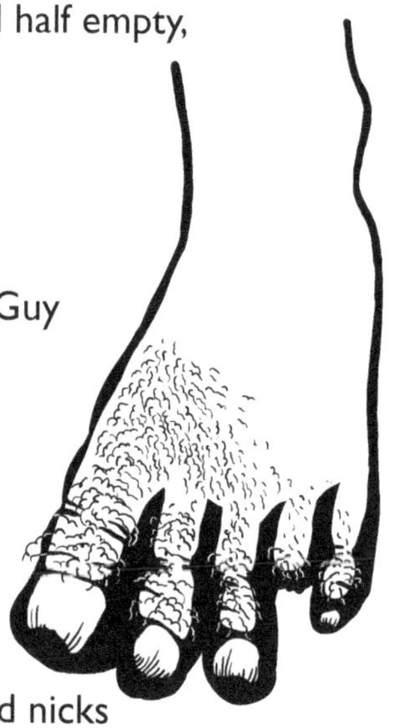

Bye bye hairbrush bye bye dandruff bye bye Tony and Guy
with your hairdressing prizes and qualified stylists,
we'll bring back the pate for the man and his mate
and no more quips about quiffs and teds and brylcreem heads
and tufts and spikes and Mohican's pillows...
no more belly-laughs
at Bobby Charlton's or waxing backs and cracks and sacks
and the weeping at the ripping of the strips in inconvenient dips and nicks
or the eye-popping combover artwork that catches us out every time...

It's all over for the hair all over!

We won't need words for alopecia, depilatory or widow's peaks
or pubic troughs or geezers doing girls' jobs with tweezers
who're getting more and more out of conditioner
and things dished up discreetly like toupées
for toffs, high-maintenance power-merkins
or nicely woven wigs from Axminster
or wasting time naming the bits we find
when we clean round the bog seats

Bye bye dumb blondes and five-inch pubes and ginger mingers
famous brazilians and unfeasible 'taches and eyebrows that meet
on both sides of the head like some irritating pop singers

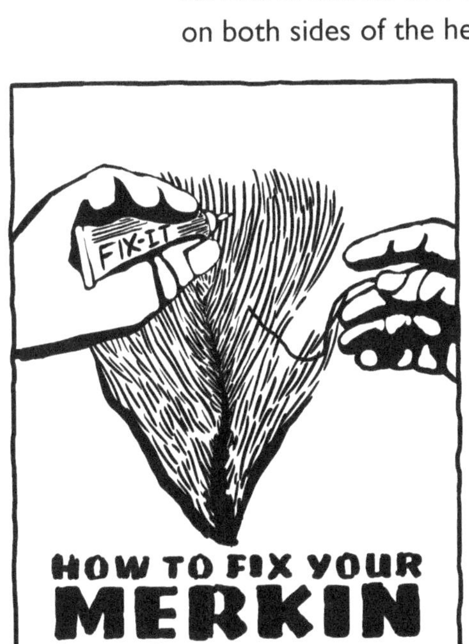

Say tara to ear hair, flat hair, mutton chops and sideburns
and school nurses warring with hairlice
and we can veto the afro, the pageboy and pelmet
and Bill Oddie's beard will be on display
in the Hide in the Sky
for all the kids to get scared at...

Say hello to smooth skulls, make friends with your pate...
hair is a sin,
hell will freeze over before hairdressers retrain
hair is cliché,
hair is wrong
hair was slick but now it's gone

No more jokes about Mary Hinge or the little fox at the Old Bull and Bush,
no more films about American men in suits one minute
and hirsute werewolves in hotel rooms hareing round our capital the next,
no more sell-out hardman big girls' perms rockers concerts in too-tight
pants looking butch.

Hair is cliché, hair is wrong,
hair was slick but now it's gone,
say hi to the beehive for the very last time
an end of frazzle for those with frizzle
and in high dudgeon, I poseth the question,
'Why wearest thou the coxcomb?'
to the ancient and his ponytail and evaporating hairline.

Nothing's bare on earth,
the world bears hair
but there's still very few
who can bear the beard.

Culled will be the mullets in their herds.
Under reduced helmets ice hockey players will chase the puck.
The King of Shaves will be soon the Knave or Knerds.
Aftershave is, was and always will be Scotch mist
and kids will wander the earth
in eternal yuletide grail in search of a decent pressie for their dads.

I have not sung of small mops, big bobs, ingrowning toe hairs or dreads
left the ceratin and silvikrin to worthier poets
let the gangland rappers sing youth's dreams of rollers and depilatory creams
sad rockers will be left shaking their pointless manes
and talk fondly of the warthair, nipple hair and Days of Immac

Know this well:
the best of hair should be kept within
a new theme for country and western tunes,
one last lament at the last wisp saloons
or fresh hope when a child is born with a four-inch tuft.

Recession for
the modern Samson,
an exchange rate
of strand to pate
it's plummeting,
there's a one man panic:
nothing to do
but comb and wait.

Beige Days

We all have heroes, we've all put up pinups, we've all wore their clothes, tried their hairstyles, but when we look back at some of our heroes there are some we come to laugh at fondly, some we come to regret and deny we ever knew and some we simply find we have become them… for me it was Gary Glitter, Margaret Thatcher and Captain Birdseye, but not in that order. I will leave you to work out which one I regret most. These were my beige days, a poem of youth, heroism and Carry On films…

Heroes and pinups pasted on the walls
watching all my furtive moves
never spoken to any real girls,
fourteen, in my beige room…

Che, The Beatles, Led Zep or The Stones…
remote, just big names, didn't fit in
not like the Duke of Effing,
the king of comedy and masculinity,
El Sid the Mighty, Emperor of my beige days,
poster king of suburbia and the nineteen-seventies:
Gladstone Screwer, Big Dick Turpin,
Sid Marks (phnarr, phnarr) the successfully sexual Sid James…

Oh, the seventies, the blousy peak of our campy times
the last ooze of innuendo squeezed out the tube of smut –
think back to all that coming out and coming on –
Dana on Top of the Pops followed by The Damned,
perms and 'taches and shrunken shorts

playing footer in the park in two-tone platform shoes and two parkas for goals
before Macdos and paedos and bricklike mobile phones
when Shankley, Bremner and the Bay City Rollers
were not so tatty, ripped and sellotaped on walls:
posters, idols, legends, but just distant big names…

Sergeant Nocker, Sidney Fiddler, the Rumpo Kid
not roles or acts but ways of being
to me, fourteen, so beige:
Big Dick Turpin, Gladstone Screwer, Sid Marks (phnarr phnarr) and El Sid:
the magnificently male
Sid James.

Refusing meat paste sandwiches on Mother's Pride in a cagoule, on a Filey family holiday,
innocence and violence and running with the deckchairs
as the yobo gangs gathered, fighting in waves down the beach
I stare transfixed as the scarves round the wrist get tangled up in punches and screams
Mum drags my innocent awe behind her
and home still dumbstruck to Bradford and the Yorkshire Ripper
Spacehoppers, Raleigh Choppers, The Reverend Flasher, Sidney Bliss
I'm fourteen, never kissed,
while all my mates are watching Clint as Dirty Harry
I whisper all your many names,
Big Dick Turpin, Gladstone Screwer, Sid Marks (phnarr phnarr) Vic Flange:
I know I am the lovechild of Sidney James.

And now nearly 40 years on, Old Sid,
not much left to say, but: I say, I say, I say…
no Effing this or Effing that in those days
you're probably turning over into other women's graves
whilst my beige has turned to grey
and nowadays all my walls are blank
except for you
and blutak, Sidney, blutak:
I've recently worked out that most of us
are not much more than bits of blue rubberised glue.

Twelve Poems About Mint

Sniffing my fingers in spring, on Menthe,
hill of Mint, me inept and following my nose
and Leake following Pausanias, obsessed by gods
all three of us enveloped here by oregano,
spikes and thyme. I'm here for the myth
and on the edge of Arcadia the lowest of the low.
Going back, I've spent all this time going back
and ended here with hands drenched in herbs
and brushed with cuts that I can't wipe clear.
These are what we were. Ordinary stories
of the commonplace telling us what we saw
before us was how to see ourselves
but we then lived on without telling much truth.
On my knees in Greece I found the raw mint.
Sniffing my fingers I can still smell the things
that won't ever leave: family, money, lies
and loveless, consuming deaths and lives
and Mother to her last breath tries and tries.

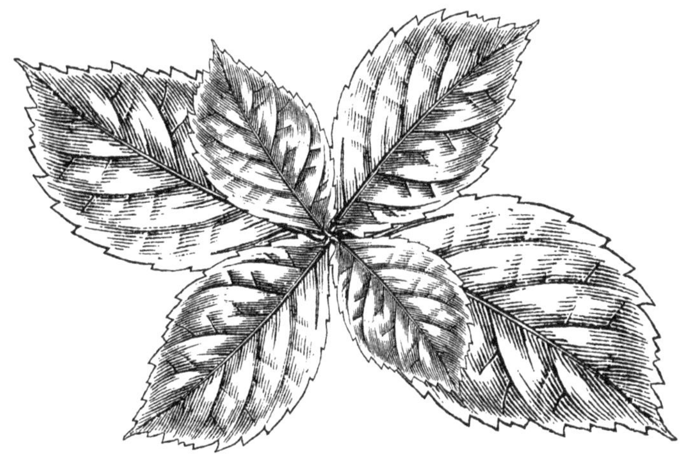

one

Usual family bollocks: daughter's
going off the rails, princessing about
matching dresses and flowers, mother's going out
of her mind at the apple of her father's

eye. And there's always blokes sniffing around.
Dirty rats, shouts Dad out the window. He
should know. He didn't know one was Hades,
helluva ladies' man who'd thrown her down

already dazzled by the nymphy bait
till Persephone from the sink estate

and hard as nails goes and smashes her face
in. Still between a rock and a hard place

she survives. Some girls do. And her sweet breath
stirs at the door to the temple of death.

1956

two

A sprig. Pretty on the plate of strudel
and ice cream, just a bit of it on the side.
Leaf-perfect symmetry, perfectly edible,
the chocolate dust like perfume just applied

and the apple tempting to contradict
on the palate mix of ripened raisins
pastry fleshy and walnuts and cool whipped
cream, she is a dream of a date with reasons,

a woman once young in a café choosing
to tempt and tease or walk away or lie

in wait for the move. She picks up the sprig,
holds it, slowly tongues it, smiles and leaves lipstick.

The thrill rasps downwards from mouth to closed thighs.
He's facing, thinks he's clever and seducing.

1959

three

So looking forward to the weekend. Not.
Dad flirting over the deep-fat fryers
on Saturday lunchtime trying old one-liners
with the girls, as if he's looking after us. Not.

Then it's aching hours suffering World of Sport
before Mum gets up to go to work. Bed and Work.
Bed and Work. Batter lingers and fish smells lurk.
She barks and wipes to rid the world of dirt.

'Do the bins, mop the floor, hoover something quick…'
And we madly do whilst Dad is inert
glued to Dr. Who, time travel takes its toll,
it's not his turn, he's northern male, a loophole
of the laws of physics. Her exhausted effort
versus gravity: frozen fishcakes, beans and chips.

1973

four

I cannot say it thrilled me, the thought of
Sunday in Goldthorpe, at Lena and Joe's,
us four squashed in the backseat with two dogs,
face to the window I stare and switch off

till lift off from the swans at New Miller Dam,
then three hours on the couch with the TV
on and Uncle Joe rattling, on sick leave
from t'pit, drags me to get summat for t'lamb:

we come back with the green prize, needs washing,
the smell lasts on hands, whilst Lena's sweating
serving and eating dinner, Mum's got that
smile nurses sometimes have feeling the part
to play, avoiding the gravy a hint
of distaste. I sniff my fingers and still cringe.

1975

five

Rimini sounds like magic when you're twelve
in the year of our bankruptcy, nineteen
seventy five, the name in my ears' shell
ringing like real lines alive from Latin

learnt with love, Rimini, the word overheard
in the holiday planning family
parley and all winter I daren't breathe a word
for fear of tearing summer's dream, Rimini,

history, Italy, Pax Romana
Augustus in his triumph and Christina

pretty aunt and beaten weak wife on the phone
sisters and husbands and love set in stone

she can't make him see. Where to if not Rimini?
Who knows, maybe nowhere. Blackpool. Filey.

1976

six

Dickens coined it: minted. His intricacies
inherited as Prince of Marshalsea
on the shore and ebb of untidy poverty,
old England's odours of injustices.

Fresh with bellyaching lack he cut his cloth
from the fish-head stalls, the barefoot night flits
ghosts of rented rooms, terror of debt and writs
tasted in greasy inn grub broth. 'From cot

to shroud,' Dickens tells her in our kitchen,
'station's hand in glove with money, love, don't doubt.

You're damned to work'. But he's disturbed the rows.
The Dodger's in there, victim of the marriage vows

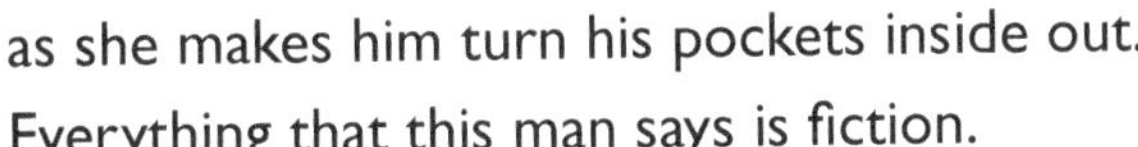

as she makes him turn his pockets inside out.
Everything that this man says is fiction.

1986

seven

The public toilet is more real than the town,
large white wall tiles, red floor, institutional
decor imaginable and emotional
in vivid, pissy, deathbed bogs in Swindon.

Gagging for air, mum's doped, her lost son gone,
stupefied husband, my uncle, cradling younger
ones, the post-mortem house in shocking slumber
of silence, numb as the autopsy they've done.

Only once months after the delayed funeral
when the second son with special needs merrily
reveals his hushed-up brother's terrible needs:

spat out squaddie at twenty-two and squatter's misdeeds,
babies with habits, popping, injecting, sniffing.
The taleteller breathes chewing gum whiffs.

1987

eight

If Lady Di had done a hard day's work
and my mum had swanned about doing nowt
and the tall posh toff had wiped some arses
would the world have loved the other woman

and worshipped her for smiling, that's work –
shirking, in my book, never get owt for nowt
we were taught, but she were a pain in't arse,
now a gobby cow from a beautiful swan,

reason I'm telling you all this is work
Mum did I did once, and jesus there's nowt

like lifting the old gimmers' sheets with shit
swimming round a bag o' bones then breathe it

in and wipe it down that's what she did for nowt
much, but she did both, dignity and work.

1989

ninc

‘Coarse. The stem’s square, fibrous, woody and thick, needs hacking
back, ‘cos it gets everywhere’ – I’m paraphrasing,
not getting much back – ‘deeply-rooted but invasive,
the leaf yields from close-up an aromatic

thwack, even before its purpley dark-brown surface
brittle and veined, almost prematurely aged
with human brown spots, sharp too at the edge
like tiny saw-teeth, pointy, jagged is

touched, then rubbed and crushed’ – I look up – glasses, stem, book –
most can’t bear much detail, listening’s hard, stem-pairing

and the metaphor of leaves as tenants on floors
withers, so the more that’s there just gets stuck

somewhere, genetic facts insolubly impairing.
Mint isn’t intricate. Likes wet soil. Everything’s coarse.

1993

ten

Such a laugh we had, all aled up, a bit
daft, the stuffiness of hellos to rellies
not well-known all blown away, good fellows
with beer bellies or illnesses desperate

in a kind way to join the flow or be
the heart and soul the night before the funeral,
laughing in the fuckin fug of fags not unusual
for the sixty cigs a day dependency

of a Dad and a dead Mam, now a scary
stiff in a chapel of rest, this knees-up

her vigil, the widower, the joker, the focus
of loss and forced, gross bonhomie, doesn't cease

for what's missing, as Dad says, 'I should've
married a woman like Mariah Carey.'

1999

eleven

Mum's on the shelf, in an unmarked wooden box,
out of sight while I decide. I'd planned a bench
round the walnut tree, like a mini-monument
but I've never settled, never quite pulled up my socks.

This long stay is her second turn abroad, her makeshift
urn in transit, through Bohemia, my rich-soiled
stop til the wild fields are boxed or feel old
and restlessness sprouts: poppy-faced, sunflower-sized, herb-thick.

Horizons were her bane, attachments her aims.
To root her children. Routines spinning round Sundays.

We, trimmed in uniform and Catholic chants,
she in her Nurse's long night's self-sacrifice.

Then, the catalogue of appointment times,
white rooms, not good news: pills to pills, fags to ashes,

she just holds her gaze, liberated, doesn't notice
the stale, clotting, kill-all disinfectants.

2004

twelve

Try it at home: squeeze an orange rind near
a naked flame and you will see it flare,
limonenes igniting through the air
from skin to oil then fire and disappear.

A lifetime's reading and I know nothing
re-infused with every sentence re-read
and the same old question brought to my slow head:
why mint? I can't wash my hands of some things.

Take the mint as if just picked and distil
gently, don't boil, with steam. Mint leaves are oil,

and water and oil are immiscible.
The same things in mint are medicinal

as oranges, help penetrate the skin.
Distil to grasp oranges are almost mint.

2015

About the Authors

Richard has carried plastic bags full of poetry books and his own poems carefully screened from members of the public for years and years until it became necessary to speak them in alcoholic auditoria in order to encourage more enjoyment in all areas of his life. This has proved so successful he is now tee-total and carries see-through plastic bags. He hopes there is more to come but can never be sure.

James takes inspiration for his drawings from individuals on the N136 night bus that goes through Camberwell. His quirky style perfectly matches Richard's wonderful poetic concoctions. This is their first collaboration. Let's hope there will be many more.

Thanks and Acknowledgements

I have to begin with a huge thank you to Mr George Messo of Red Hand Books without whose inspiring thoughts and extraordinariness this book would never have happened: truly, a big thank you. And to Carole, my wife, the finest of readers and loveliest of people. And to Mr Simon Kelly who has listened to this stuff for years and years and still puts up with me. And to Mr James Castleden, a truly gifted artist who has added so much (laughter) in the making of this book. And to pln for too many things to put on paper.

RDE

I must thank Richard Eccles for entrusting me with the job of illustrating these works of art. His endless encouragement and ability to imagine the final product from the most incomplete of red-coloured sketches is testimony to his genius. A big thank you to my ever-patient wife, Ivett, who understands me better than anyone. And thank you to my parents, patrons of my arts from the age of five.

James Castleden

Sending in Thong Poems

If you're inspired to write your own thong poem, we'd love to hear from you. E-mail us at poemsfromtheplasticbag@yahoo.co.uk.

www.rhbks.com

www.ingramcontent.com/pod-product-compliance
Ingram Content Group UK Ltd.
Pitfield, Milton Keynes, MK11 3LW, UK
UKHW062003290726
14090UKWH00022B/1356

9 781910 346136